W9-COG-122

A TRUE BOOK™

Food Allergies

WITHDRAWN

CHRISTINE TAYLOR-BUTLER

Children's Press®
An Imprint of Scholastic Inc.
New York Toronto London Auckland Sydney
Mexico City New Delhi Hong Kong
Danbury, Connecticut

Content Consultant

Lawrence J. Cheskin, M.D., F.A.C.P.
Associate Professor,
Johns Hopkins Bloomberg School of Public Health
The Johns Hopkins University
Baltimore, Maryland

Library of Congress Cataloging-in-Publication Data

Taylor-Butler, Christine.
  Food allergies / by Christine Taylor-Butler.
       p. cm. -- (A true book)
  Includes index.
     ISBN-13: 978-0-531-16858-5 (lib. bdg.)
              978-0-531-20732-1 (pbk.)
     ISBN-10: 0-531-16858-1 (lib. bdg.)
              0-531-20732-3 (pbk.)
  1. Food allergy in children--Juvenile literature. I. Title.
II. Series.

  RJ386.5.T39 2008
  618.92'975--dc22   2007036016

No part of this publication may be reproduced in whole or in part, or stored in a retrieval system, or transmitted in any form or by any means, electronic, mechanical, photocopying, recording, or otherwise, without written permission of the publisher. For information regarding permission, write to Scholastic Inc., 557 Broadway, New York, NY 10012.

Produced by Weldon Owen Education Inc.

©2008 Scholastic Inc.

All rights reserved. Published in 2008 by Children's Press, an imprint of Scholastic Inc.
Published simultaneously in Canada. Printed in China. 62
SCHOLASTIC, CHILDREN'S PRESS, A TRUE BOOK, and associated logos are trademarks and/or registered trademarks of Scholastic Inc.

1 2 3 4 5 6 7 8 9 10 R 17 16 15 14 13 12 11 10 09 08

Find the Truth!

Everything you are about to read is true *except* for one of the sentences on this page.

Which one is **TRUE**?

T or F   You can get an allergic reaction just from smelling fish.

T or F   There is a cure for food allergies.

Find the answers in this book.

Contents

Wheat flour can cause an allergic reaction if it gets into the air.

CHAPTER 1

A Rash Decision?

It's time for lunch. You open your lunch bag. You pull out a turkey sandwich and a bottle of water. A friend offers you a sugar cookie. You know that peanuts make you sick. Sugar cookies aren't made with peanuts though. It looks tempting. You take a bite. Is this a **rash decision**?

About two million U.S. schoolchildren are allergic to at least one food.

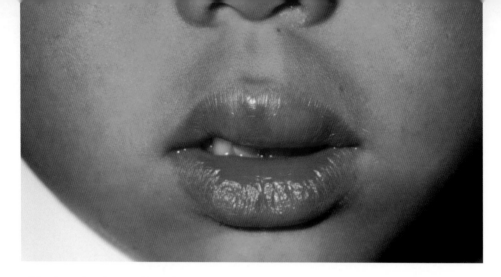

This boy had an allergic reaction to peanuts. His lips swelled.

Within minutes of eating the cookie, you feel ill. There must have been traces of peanuts in it. Your mouth starts to tingle. Your throat swells. You have difficulty breathing. Your hands develop a rash. What's going on?

You're having an allergic reaction. You're not alone. Many people suffer from allergies. Allergies are harmful reactions that the body has to a substance, such as food. There is a way to avoid harm. You should avoid the thing that causes the allergy.

301

ALLERGY WARNING

NO PEANUTS OR NUTS
ALLOWED IN THIS AREA

Some schools ban peanuts
and nuts altogether. Allergy
warning signs remind
the students and teachers.

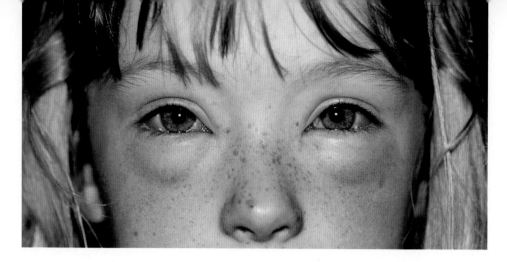

A mild allergic reaction can cause swollen, watery eyes.

Allergic Reactions

Sometimes the symptoms of an allergic reaction are mild. There may simply be a rash or a mild itch. Sometimes the reaction is more serious. The person may require hospital treatment.

People with food allergies try to avoid the foods that make them ill. But often the danger is hidden. A person may eat something that has come into contact with another food. Even touching or smelling a certain food could set off an allergic reaction.

Remember that cookie? It didn't contain peanuts. But it had been in a lunch bag with a peanut butter and jelly sandwich. Some of the peanut butter was on your friend's hands when he handed you the cookie. Even a tiny amount can spell danger!

Peanuts are the most common cause of death from food allergies.

Hay fever is a common allergy. People with hay fever often sneeze. It is the body's way of getting rid of foreign substances in the nose.

CHAPTER 2

When the Body Attacks

Many people think that allergies are caused only by things such as dust, pollen, pets, and even molds. Food is good for you, isn't it? How can the body react badly to something good?

Some people are allergic to the dandruff of a pet!

Some Allergy Symptoms

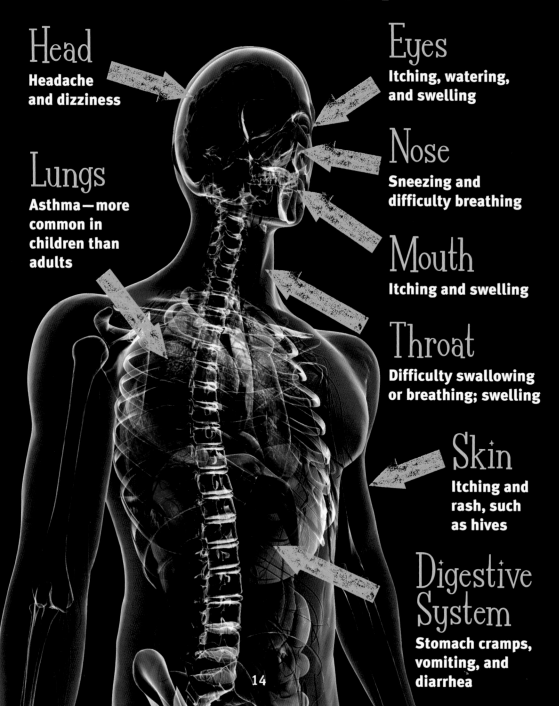

Head
Headache and dizziness

Lungs
Asthma—more common in children than adults

Eyes
Itching, watering, and swelling

Nose
Sneezing and difficulty breathing

Mouth
Itching and swelling

Throat
Difficulty swallowing or breathing; swelling

Skin
Itching and rash, such as hives

Digestive System
Stomach cramps, vomiting, and diarrhea

Food and the Body

Food allergies are not a normal response to eating. They are triggered by your **immune** system. When you are allergic to something, your body registers that food as being a dangerous foreign invader. It launches a defense to get rid of it.

When you eat, your body breaks down food. It extracts nutrients. These are absorbed into your bloodstream. Your body contains **antibodies** called **immunoglobulin** E (IgE). These tiny molecules circulate in your blood. In people with food allergies, these antibodies are programmed to attack specific food proteins. IgE molecules attach to certain cells in the body, such as those in your nose and throat. They wait for an invader to arrive. The invader may arrive in a mouthful of milk.

An **allergen** is a substance that triggers an allergic reaction. An allergen, such as a milk protein, has molecules on its surface. These are called **antigens**. An IgE antibody with a perfect fit for a milk antigen attaches to that antigen. This triggers certain cells to release a chemical into your body. The chemical is called **histamine**. Histamine can cause your body to break out in a rash. Your skin may develop a severe itch and swelling, called hives. As the milk protein travels through your digestive system, it may trigger other reactions. These can include vomiting, stomach cramps, and diarrhea. Most symptoms resolve within 36 to 72 hours.

A mosquito bite can cause swelling and itching. This is an example of a histamine reaction.

This artwork shows a mast cell. Mast cells and some white blood cells contain histamine. Histamine is released from these cells in response to an allergen.

Antigen

Antibody

Histamine

Wheat
This can be hiding in frankfurters.

Milk
This can be hiding in canned tuna.

Soybeans
These can be hiding in peanut butter.

Fish
This can be hiding in salad dressings.

Shellfish
This can be hiding in steak sauce.

18

Hidden Danger!

Eight foods cause 90 percent of all food allergies. These are eggs, milk, nuts, peanuts, fish, shellfish, soybeans, and wheat. Sometimes they can be found in other food products.

Eggs

These can be hiding in marshmallows.

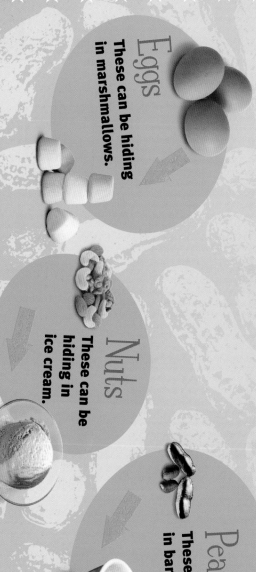

Nuts

These can be hiding in ice cream.

Peanuts

These can be hiding in barbecue sauce.

19

CHAPTER 3

The Government in Action

Have you ever looked at the ingredients list on a food package? You would if you had a food allergy. In the past, labels were not very clear. A label might list casein. This is the main protein found in milk. It might list albumin. This is a protein found in egg whites. Both of these proteins can trigger allergic reactions.

In the past, there were about 20 different ways to label milk.

Food Safety

How do you tell whether or not a food is safe for you? The federal government has departments that are responsible for keeping our food supply safe. The Food and Drug Administration (FDA) is responsible for making safety rules. The rules are for seafood, fruits, vegetables, and other non-meat products.

For some people, vegetables and fruits can be harmful. These foods can come into contact with an allergen.

The FDA does not require labeling for fresh fruits and vegetables.

USDA scientists explore many aspects of agriculture. These include research on crop nutrition and crop production.

The U.S. Department of Agriculture (USDA) is responsible for eggs, meat, and dairy products. The FDA and USDA work with farmers and food manufacturers. They ensure that food is safe and properly labeled. They inspect processing plants. They set standards for the food industry.

Clear and Simple

The FDA set out to make the food supply safe. It met with people who had allergic reactions to food. This helped the FDA create better rules for food labels. In 2004, the FDA required food manufacturers to use the common names for foods on their labels. Manufacturers were told to use language that a child could understand.

The labeling rule applies to the eight foods that cause most food allergies. But there are still problems. The rule doesn't apply to other foods. These foods cause the remaining ten percent of all allergic reactions.

Salicylate is a natural chemical. It occurs in tomatoes and strawberries. Some people are allergic to it.

Names for Food

Food labels list ingredients and provide nutrition information. Labels use easy language. They may also contain allergy warnings. However, a common food allergen may have different uncommon names. For instance, milk can have the uncommon names casein or lactose.

Names for wheat:
- semolina
- gluten
- bulgur
- graham flour
- couscous
- kamut
- durum
- spelt
- farina
- bran

Names for eggs:
- albumin
- meringue
- conalbumin
- ovalbumin
- ovomucin
- ovomucoid
- globulin
- ovovitellin
- livetin
- vitellin

Labeling Correctly

Labeling a food correctly is more complicated than it may seem. If equipment has been used to process peanuts, a tiny trace of peanuts may remain on the machine. The machine may then be used to process another food. A tiny trace of the peanuts may get into that food. This may threaten the life of someone who has a peanut allergy. So the label on the food must state that the product "may contain traces of peanuts."

Food Laws Time Line

1907
Federal Meat Inspection Act begins.

1939
Food standards issued for canned tomatoes, tomato puree, and tomato paste.

If a food is found to contain a substance that is not properly marked on the label, the government can require a recall. That means that the public must be told of the danger. People can bring the product back for a full refund or replacement.

Not all foods come from the United States. So FDA scientists and inspectors work to make sure foods imported from other countries are also tested and properly labeled.

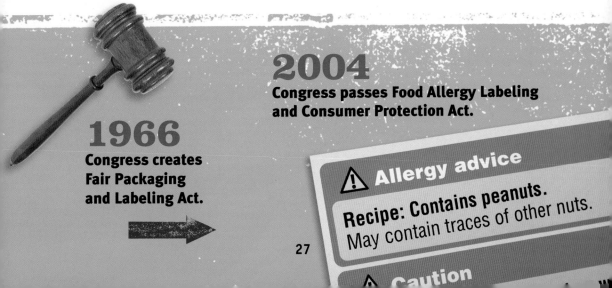

2004
Congress passes Food Allergy Labeling and Consumer Protection Act.

1966
Congress creates Fair Packaging and Labeling Act.

⚠ **Allergy advice**

Recipe: Contains peanuts.
May contain traces of other nuts.

⚠ **Caution**

CHAPTER **4**

Allergy Detective

A fish market can be a dangerous place. Just the smell of fish can cause an allergic reaction in some people!

Some people know right away when a food makes them ill. For others, the cause of an allergic reaction is a mystery. It requires some detective work. A doctor will ask what the person ate and even what he or she touched before becoming sick. The doctor is likely to do some tests. It is possible to be allergic to more than one food.

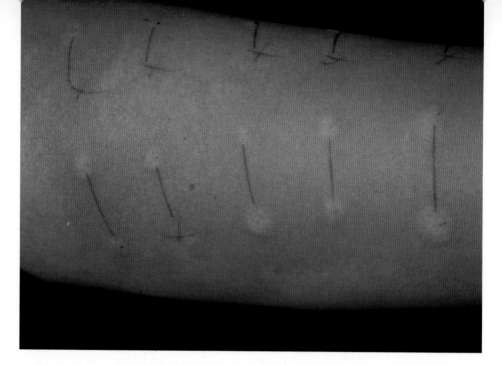

Skin tests are often done on a person's arm or back.

Allergy Tests

The easiest allergy test is a skin prick. Drops of fluid containing different allergens are placed beneath the skin. If the person is allergic to a substance, the skin will become red and slightly swollen. This is called a positive reaction. The test may produce no reaction at all.

Sometimes doctors eliminate foods from a person's diet. The foods are then reintroduced to the diet in a controlled way. Some people undergo food challenge tests. They eat foods that they suspect might cause allergic reactions. A doctor carefully monitors the effects that different food allergens have on the person.

This boy is undergoing a food challenge test.

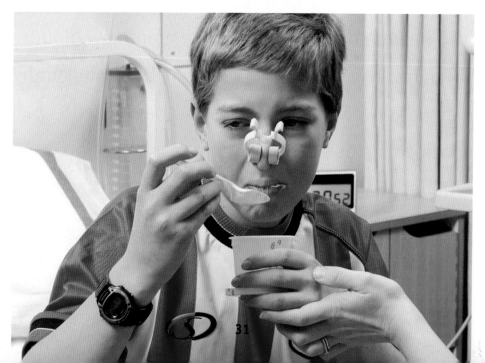

31

Mild to Severe

Allergic reactions range from mild to severe. Mild allergic reactions can be treated with drugs, such as **antihistamines**. These can be bought at a pharmacy. A doctor may also prescribe a **steroid** cream. This soothes some symptoms.

The most severe kind of reaction is called **anaphylactic shock**. This is a rare allergic reaction. It affects a person's whole body. Symptoms include skin rashes and wheezing. They also include tightness in the chest and low blood pressure. The person has difficulty breathing and may pass out. In extreme cases, anaphylactic shock can cause death. Emergency first aid is required. Doctors treat anaphylactic shock with oxygen and **epinephrine**. Two out of 1,000 allergy sufferers die from anaphylactic shock.

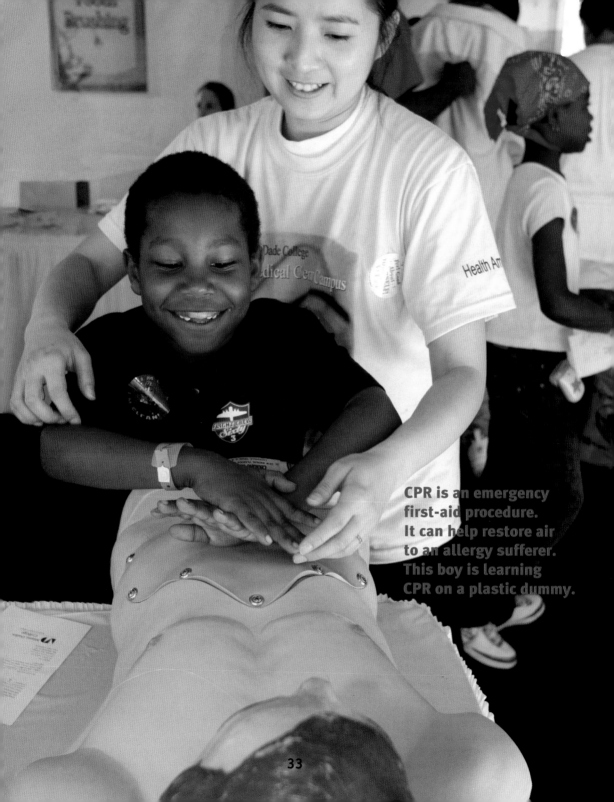

CPR is an emergency
first-aid procedure.
It can help restore air
to an allergy sufferer.
This boy is learning
CPR on a plastic dummy.

Be on the Alert

Some allergic reactions can lead to a life-or-death situation. Minutes count. If you have an allergy, remember to take responsibility for your own health. Many severe allergy sufferers carry an EpiPen with them at all times. This is a self-injecting syringe that releases epinephrine. This hormone is also called adrenalin. Epinephrine relaxes the muscles in the lung's air passages. It helps restore breathing.

Many allergy sufferers wear a medical alert bracelet or necklace. These explain what allergies the person has. They explain how to help the person if there is a problem.

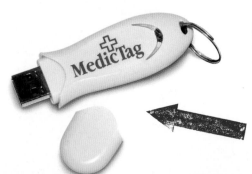

Some medical alert devices have a computer chip. This stores medical information.

This doctor is talking to an allergy sufferer about an EpiPen. Some people practice using EpiPens by injecting an orange.

Having a severe allergy doesn't mean that you can't lead an enjoyable life. You just have to be prepared. This girl carries her EpiPen everywhere.

CHAPTER 5

Staying Healthy

EpiPens are for emergency use. They can be used only once.

Allergies often develop in childhood. Some people grow out of their allergies. But many do not. If you have a food allergy, finding safe and healthy food choices can be a challenge. Eating out at a restaurant or at a friend's place can be difficult. However, there are ways to stay safe.

Allergy Awareness

Many people still do not know about food allergies. They may not be aware that a common food can harm some people. They may not know that being touched by someone who has handled a certain food can cause harm. The sufferer can break out in a rash—or worse. If you have an allergy, let people know about it. Tell your teacher. Let people in your school cafeteria know too.

Contamination!

Ask questions when you go out to eat. When you go out for ice cream, ask the server to use a clean scoop. If you are allergic to strawberries, you don't want your vanilla ice cream dipped with the same scoop that was dipped in the strawberry ice cream!

If you have a milk allergy, ask the deli not to slice meat for your sandwich with the same equipment they use to slice cheese. Don't eat bagels or pretzels if you have an egg allergy. Egg whites may have been used to make them shiny.

If you are preparing food at home, clean work surfaces thoroughly with soap and water. This helps prevent cross-contamination. Rinsing with water alone does not remove a food allergen.

Calcium-fortified orange juice is a good substitute for milk.

Choose Substitutes

It is important to eat a healthy, balanced diet. People with food allergies must look for foods that can provide the same nutrition as the foods they can't eat. For instance, milk is an important source of calcium. Calcium helps build strong bones. Leafy green vegetables are high in calcium. These include spinach. They are a good substitute for milk.

There are many recipes available that show you how to cook without ingredients that cause an allergic reaction. For instance, you can often use juice instead of milk when baking. You can substitute plain gelatin and water for an egg.

You can substitute wheat flour with flour made from rye, oats, barley, or rice.

Sharing Meals Together

Food is a big part of everyday life. It is fun to be able to share meals with friends and family at a picnic or a party. However, if you have an allergy, it is important to be careful. You should eat only food that you have checked over. By taking sensible precautions, people with food allergies can live long and healthy lives! ★

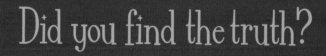

Percentage of children who will develop an allergy if both their parents have an allergy:
About 75 percent

Number of foods that cause allergies:
About 160

Number of people in the United States with food allergies: About 11 million

Number of people in the United States who die from food allergies each year: About 150

Number of emergency room visits due to food allergies: About 30,000 per year

Did you find the truth?

T You can get an allergic reaction just from smelling fish.

F There is a cure for food allergies.

Resources

Books

Ballard, Carol. *Special Diets and Food Allergies* (Making Healthy Food Choices). Portsmouth, NH: Heinemann, 2007.

Gordon, Sherri Mabry. *Peanut Butter, Milk, and Other Deadly Threats*. Berkeley Heights, NJ: Enslow Publishers, 2006.

Schlosser, Eric and Charles Wilson. *Chew On This: Everything You Don't Want to Know About Fast Food*. New York: Houghton Mifflin, 2006.

Silverstein, Dr. Alvin and Virginia, and Laura Silverstein Nunn. *Allergies* (My Health Series). New York: Franklin Watts, 1999.

Taylor-Butler, Christine. *Food Safety* (A True Book™: Health and the Human Body). New York: Children's Press, 2008.

Weiner, Ellen. *Taking Food Allergies to School*. Plainview, NY: Jayjo Books, 1999.

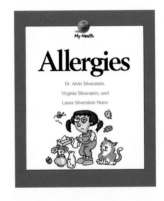

Organizations and Web Sites

Food Allergy Web Site

www.fankids.org
Find out how the body reacts to a food allergen.

FDA Center for Food Safety and Applied Nutrition

www.cfsan.fda.gov/~dms/ffalrgn.html
The Food and Drug Administration's site for information
on food allergens.

Meals for You

www.mealsforyou.com/cgi-bin/advancedSearch?term=
Click on the foods that you wish to avoid, then search
for recipes.

Place to Visit

ARS National Visitor Center

Powder Mill Road
Beltsville, MD 20705
301-504-9403
www.ars.usda.gov/is/nvc
Tour the visitor center for the
USDA's Agriculture Research Service,
where you can learn about food
science and nutrition.

Important Words

allergen (AL-ur-jin) – a substance that causes an allergic reaction

anaphylactic shock – a life-threatening reaction to an allergen

antibody (AN-ti-bod-ee) – a protein that attacks invaders in the body

antigen (AN-ti-jin) – a substance on an allergen that recognizes and binds to an antibody

antihistamine (an-tie-HISS-tuh-meen) – a drug that combats the effect of histamine

epinephrine (eh-puh-NEH-frin) – a hormone created to help the body cope in times of stress

histamine – a compound released by cells to combat allergens. It causes the symptoms of an allergy.

immune (i-MYOON) – resistant to an infection or a foreign substance

immunoglobulin – a tiny molecule in the body that helps identify and destroy foreign invaders. It is also known as an antibody.

rash decision – a decision made quickly and without much thought

steroid (STAIR-oid) – a chemical substance found naturally

Index

Page numbers in **bold** indicate illustrations

About the Author

Christine Taylor-Butler lives in Kansas City, Missouri, with her husband and two daughters. A native of Ohio, she is the author of more than 40 books for children. She holds a B.S. degree in both Civil Engineering and Art and Design from the Massachusetts Institute of Technology in Cambridge, MA. Other books by Ms. Taylor-Butler in the True Book Health and the Human Body series include: *The Food Pyramid*, *Food Safety*, *The Circulatory System*, *The Respiratory System*, *The Digestive System*, and *The Nervous System*.

PHOTOGRAPHS: Big Stock Photo (flour, p. 5; peanuts, p. 11; mosquito, p. 16; various foods, pp. 18–19; © Lori Sparkia, sandwich, p. 11); Courtesy of www.medictag.com (p. 34); Getty Images (p. 6; p. 14; p. 30; p. 38; p. 41); Ingram Image Library (back cover, p. 5; p. 22; p. 24; p. 27); iStockPhoto.com (p. 4; p. 21; ice cream, p. 39; © Daniel Tero, cover); Photodisc (p. 13); Photolibrary (p. 8; p. 10; p. 12; p. 17; p. 20; p. 27; p. 31; p. 33; pp. 35–36); Stock.XCHNG (p. 43); Tranz: Corbis (p. 9; p. 23; p. 26; p. 40; p. 42); Reuters (p. 28). All other images property of Weldon Owen Education.